A JAPANESE BOY SEES A NEW LIGHT

Escaping from
NORTH KOREA

SHU SHIMIZU

PARTRIDGE

Library of Congress Control Number: 2022913945
ISBN: Hardcover   978-1-5437-7097-1
                    Softcover   978-1-5437-7095-7
                    eBook   978-1-5437-7096-4

Print information available on the last page.

To order additional copies of this book, contact
Toll Free +65 3165 7531 (Singapore)
Toll Free +60 3 3099 4412 (Malaysia)
orders.singapore@partridgepublishing.com

www.partridgepublishing.com/singapore

In memory of Father

PREFACE

As I write, seventy-five years have passed since Japan lost the war against the United States. And now it is in the middle of the worldwide coronavirus crisis, and my supplementary private English school has been closed nearly for two years. This nothing-to-do situation triggered me to write down my experiences and the thoughts I had while escaping from North Korea to South Korea over a period of the nine months. "How do I write these?" was a big question. I first began to write in a diary format from the point of view of my nine-year-old self, a Japanese boy journaling from time to time as his family made their way from the newly created North Korea finally to arrive in Seoul, South Korea. That effort was the genesis of this memoir.

There are many books in Japanese that describe the experiences of Japanese refugees as they escaped from

North Korea to South Korea, but this perspective is less known in English, so I decided to write such a book. I hope my story will be read by my relatives and friends who understand English in Japan and by my cousins' family members in Brazil—and of course by my friends in America as well.

Why do I have friends in the United States? For forty years, I lived there—in San Diego, San Francisco, Dallas, Columbus, and Las Vegas. I came back to Japan twenty years ago. I was married but didn't have any children. I now live alone in Nagoya, the capital city of Aichi Prefecture, next to Shizuoka Prefecture.

Incidentally you will find two names signed by Toru and Shu on the illustrations throughout this book. Toru who was my eldest brother had written a book in Japanese in 1980 about his experiences escaping from North Korea to South Korea. Out of his book I borrowed some illustrations drawn by him, and used our family pictures which his son possessed. Those illustrations signed by Shu are my own drawings.

CONTENTS

1

THE WAR AND THE EMPEROR

"Ugh!" Father moaned, hitting the tatami mat floor with his fists and crying out, "We've been defeated!"

Tears were flowing down his cheeks, and his hands were shaking. Mother was crying, too, with her hand on his shoulder. My older brother Yoshi whispered to me, "Shu, Japan has just lost the war."

We were listening to the voice from the radio on the table. The voice from the radio was Emperor Hirohito's. It was August 15, 1945. The words which the Emperor was using were too difficult for me. I was only nine years old. I must have looked puzzled, so Yoshi explained to me what was happening.

We lived in Kisshu, a northern city of the Korean Peninsula. Yoshi and I were enjoying our summer vacation at home. Father had taken a short break and had come home from the Kisshu Locomotive Yard nearby in order to listen to the Emperor's special speech. We were sitting straight up on the tatami floor.

August 15, 1945

"Stand up straight or sit up straight when you hear the word 'emperor.'" That was the way we were taught in school. That was why Yoshi and I were sitting straight up listening to the Emperor's speech.

The war against America had started the same year I entered elementary school in the city of Seishin, located in the north of Kisshu. In the beginning of the war, a lot of soldiers were killed on both the Japanese and American sides around the Pacific Ocean. Then

Japanese islanders in Okinawa! Why didn't the Emperor end the war right then? After that, millions of civilians were killed in Tokyo, and thousands of civilians were killed in every city all over Japan. An atomic bomb killed many more people in Hiroshima, and another atomic bomb in Nagasaki! Why did the Emperor wait so late to end the war?

But the Emperor's speech finally did bring the war to an end. The Emperor was the only person who was able to end the war. Every citizen in Japan had been brainwashed to keep fighting "till the end." Those three words meant "until every one of the Japanese was killed." What an awful thought!

Before Japan could start the war against America, Prime Minister Hideki Tojo had to get the Emperor's permission. Mr. Tojo visited the Emperor' palace and asked for his permission. Then the Emperor asked Mr. Tojo if Japan should be able to defeat America. Mr. Tojo answered, "Sure thing, Your Majesty!"

That meant the Emperor started the war and ended the war. Didn't it mean that the Emperor was the number one war criminal?

Japanese people believed that the Emperor's family had controlled the nation of Japan for the last 2,600 years, not for 1,945 years. There was even a song entitled "The Era 2600," and pure Japanese blood was respected. I thought that was the reason the Japanese believed "We Japanese are superior to any other races" and started invading neighboring countries before the war.

2

MY FAMILY MEMBERS

Let me introduce myself and my family members. I'll start with myself.

Shu

I am Shu Shimizu. I was born in Keijo (Seoul) in February 1936. Keijo was the capital city of Chosen (Korea), which was governed by Japan for thirty-six years, until Japan surrendered to America on August 15, 1945. I was a boy of nine at the time, in the fourth grade at Kisshu Elementary School in the northern part of the Chosen (Korean) Peninsula.

I lived in Keijo until I was five years old. I can recall things around our house and things that happened there when I was three or four years old.

There was a wide river near the house. After dinner, Father and Mother used to take a walk along the river with me. I always walked between them, and now and then they would lift me forwards for a few seconds. I liked that very much, but I liked Father's back much better. So I pretended to be too tired to walk any farther, and Father would tell me to climb on his back. I was a go-to-bed-early type and always got sleepy on his comfortable back. Then he would tell me to stay awake.

"If you sleep, I will toss you into the river," he said. But I knew he wasn't serious. Next morning I always found myself safe on the futon.

Once there was a flood, and the rainwater came up close to the front door. I found a cute green frog floating over the doorstep.

There was a big rugby field in front of the house, and across the field there was a beautiful Japanese garden.

Evening Walk

Yoshi often took me to his kindergarten and read many children's books to me there. There were several spikes buried at the gate, and I wondered why.

Yoshi

My brother Yoshi Shimizu and I went to Kisshu Elementary School. When the war ended in 1945, he was eleven years old and in the sixth grade.

Yoshi was what we call a bookworm and often read books to me as we lay together on the *ondoru* floor (a floor heated in the Korean way). He was such a nice and kind brother to me. Although I knew that well, I often fought with him. I couldn't control my temper and would throw anything around me at him—cushions, pencils, books, teacups, or even a pair of scissors. I was the hot-tempered, spoiled baby of the family. When Father found out that I started the fight, he whipped his bamboo stick on both our rear ends. Then I would feel sorry and cry for Yoshi.

Toru

Toru was another brother of mine, fourteen years old and in his third year at a junior high school in a suburb of Seishin. Because he was a dormitory student, taking a special premilitary drill for summer there, Toru wasn't at home when the Emperor surrendered to America on the radio. He was very smart and wanted to go to Tokyo University in the future.

Toru was very quiet and a lot taller than Yoshi, so I couldn't say even a word against him. I didn't talk to him much.

At times, he went against our parents and bolted out of the house. Then Mother had to go out to look for him. Strangely, she always found him and brought him home, where he had to accept Father's bamboo-stick punishment. Yoshi and I always cried for Toru even though we had nothing to do with what he had done.

Mother

My mother's name was Suzuko Shimizu. She was only seventeen years old when she married Father. The next year Toru was born. She was a daughter of a very wealthy family, and a graduate from a prestigious high school.

In those days, not many girls went to high school in Japan. Mother had more education than Father. Her penmanship was beautiful. She was a refined and sophisticated woman—the prettiest among the students' mothers when she came to the PTA meetings. She never hit me, and she loved me a lot, while Father never showed me his love.

One of Mother's hobbies was sewing. Most of our futons and her kimonos were her own

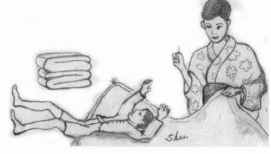

A Spoilt Child

works. They were all masterpieces. I liked rolling on the futons that she was making. Why did I do that? It was because I wanted to be in her way. She waited patiently for me to get off the half-finished futons.

That was one of my games with her, but I was not allowed to do it when she was sewing kimonos.

"Mother, is this a kimono?"

"That's right. Stay off the kimono, Shu, because sewing kimonos is very complicated, and I'm making this kimono for a friend of mine." I must have been four years old then.

Another hobby of hers was collecting fine sets of china. Since Father often had home parties for his staff members and for the neighbors who lived in the residential complex owned by the Korean Railroad Company, Mother willingly kept on buying expensive dishes. She would often sit before those dishes for minutes and admire their beauty. She also enjoyed tea ceremony, flower arrangement, and haiku. Mother was thirty-six years old when the Emperor ended the war.

Father

Father's name was Takeshi Shimizu. He was forty-two years old, born as the eighth and last baby of a farmer's family in Shizuoka Prefecture, Japan. His father had lost his life in an accident when Father was only two years old, and I heard that he had had a very hard childhood.

As soon as he finished his elementary school education, he took a job as a fireman on the locomotives of the Japan National Railroad Company. He became a locomotive driver when he was twenty years old. He worked very hard and passed the locomotive engineering test at twenty-five, and then strictly on his own transferred to Korean Railway Company, a subsidiary organization of Japan National Railroad Co. This company had been established by the Japanese government during its occupation of Korea.

At first, he was stationed at the Keijo (Seoul) Locomotive Yard. After he was settled, he made a trip to his hometown in Shizuoka Prefecture, married Mother, and started his married life in Keijo, the capital city of Chosen (Korea). We three brothers were all born in Keijo and had never visited our parents' country, Japan.

When I was five years old, Father was transferred to another locomotive yard in the city of Seishin, the year before I was to enter elementary school. Mother didn't want to move up north to the cold city by the Sea of Japan but agreed to move with him. She was very happy for her husband's promotion and his moving up the ladder in the world of the railroad company, in spite of his educational background.

Father must have been the specialist for resolving the aftermath of derailments in the northern part of Korea. When a derailment happened, he had to be there to solve the problem. Our home phone often rang during the night. He snuck out while we were asleep and didn't come home for two or three days.

After we had lived in Seishin for four years, we had to move again, following another big promotion. Father became assistant director of the Kisshu Locomotive Yard, 100 kilometers south of Seishin. It was in April, when the Japanese school year began, and Yoshi and I transferred to Kisshu Elementary School. And four months later—to be exact, on August 15, 1945—Japan lost the war.

Father in His Office

Father was very strict with himself and also too strict with his three sons. He wanted to raise us in his own Spartan way. He never used his hand but rather a narrow bamboo stick, once on our behinds in each incident that made him upset. He always kept the stick on his desk. I hated this bamboo stick and hid it once. Oh, he was mad, and my behind was hit three times instead of once.

Father was not mean to Mother. As a matter of fact, he was very sweet to her. Why was he so different? He was very friendly to his friends, his staff members, and even to total strangers, but not to his own sons.

I don't know when he learned to play the *shakuhachi*, a Japanese bamboo flute. He had shakuhachi classes at home on weekends. Once he was invited to a local radio studio and played the shakuhachi. He must have played the instrument pretty well. When he played it, our pet dog, a pointer, always howled.

When he was off duty, he had to be doing something. He went fishing and casting nets with his family. He went hunting with his pet pointer, named Passie. He actually wanted to name it Passion, but he was afraid to use the English word because of pressure to avoid English expressions.

Shu's First Summer in 1936

He often went shopping with Mother. He took us out for dinner once a month, calling it 'Mother's Night.' He meant to show his gratitude to her everyday work in the kitchen. He liked sake and often threw parties at home. When he got drunk, he turned into a total stranger: he became a very happy man, and showed a lot of love to us.

Father 38, Toru 12, Yoshi 9, Shu 6, Mother 30
1942

My Name

Mother's second childbirth was twin babies, Yoshi and Atsushi. Atsushi died before I was born. Father had wanted a girl and decided to name the next baby *Shuko* because *ko* indicates female. But his next baby was a boy ... me. So Father was very disappointed. He simply dropped the *ko* and named me *Shu* instead of *Shuko*.

Father's dream   Shuko 修子

****

Reality   修

Shu

or

Osamu

Shu

Father's Dream

When my name is written in Chinese, in Japan it is usually read as *Osamu*. So I am called Osamu when strangers read my written name. This Osamu character is pronounced *shiu* in China and *shu* in Japan.

Father once told me that the Chinese character *shu* is used for girls in China. That means Father really wanted me to be born as a girl. Sorry about that, Father! But I like the name Shu better than Osamu. It is shorter and unique. I happened to like my name Shu very much, which Father only reluctantly named me. Isn't that ironic?

3

FAREWELL

"The war ended yesterday! No more war! I didn't have to die! Hip hip hurrah!" I yelled. I just woke up and was jumping around the house. Mother and Yoshi were talking quietly. They must have been talking about our future.

Then we heard an airplane. The noise was getting louder.

"Let's see it," Yoshi said.

We opened the window, got up on the sill, and waved our hands at the airplane.

"The war is over, hurray!" I shouted.

The plane got closer.

Da, da, da! A few bullets hit our house. We saw the pilot.

"Hey, he is shooting at us!" Yoshi screamed, pushing me down to the floor. He then jumped off the windowsill and shouted, "Mother, it was a Russian plane. The war is not over. Let's hit the shelter!"

Within a minute, we were inside the shelter in the front yard. The Russian plane did not come back. What was that about?

When Father came home in the evening, he told us.

"Toru will come home late tomorrow afternoon, but we must abandon the house before that, around 14:30. Some Japanese soldiers didn't believe Japan had lost the war and shot at Russian airplanes in this city. Russia might send bombers to this city. Besides that, we Japanese are not allowed to live in Korea any longer. I'll put you on the three o'clock train for Huzan before Toru comes home. As you know, Huzan is the southernmost city of Korea, where you catch a ship to Japan."

"Why must we abandon everything? Why must we go to Japan?" I asked these questions of Mother.

"Time will tell," she answered. This was Mother's shortcut. When something was difficult to explain, Mother used this line.

That night, Father was packing his bag, and Mother was packing Toru's. Father was to carry these two bags to his office next morning and wait for Toru to come there. Next morning, Mother was to pack her own bag, Yoshi's bag, and mine. After leaving this house, we would go to Kisshu Station by 14:30 to get on the three o'clock train bound for Huzan.

If I must leave here tomorrow, I thought, I would like to say sayonara to my best friend and my homeroom teacher. They both lived in the same fenced-up living area, which was owned by a large Japanese paper mill factory. When I had visited my friend there in April, I saw apricot flowers on both sides of the roads. They were so pretty and smelled so sweet. I was envious of people living in such a luxurious environment.

My best friend, Taro Hanai, was actually Korean but went to the same Japanese school that Yoshi and I did. Korean kids were very rare in Japanese schools. The reason he could go to my school was that his father was a barber employed by the Japanese factory for employees and their families. I didn't know Taro's real Korean name, but that was not important.

The second person to visit was my beautiful homeroom teacher, Miss Miyajima, whose father was director of the paper mill factory. If I could see her together with Taro, it would be killing two birds with one stone.

The idea was OK, and it went the way I wanted. But it wasn't the right time. Her father had been abducted by several Koreans right before Taro and I visited her house. Our teacher was shaken up and couldn't say much. She kept crying. Their housekeeper told us the terrifying story. We had to leave immediately without saying our farewells.

Before Taro and I parted, he said to me, "We will have to leave this factory-owned house although we are Korean—because we are living in the Japanese community and Korean people envy us so much. I'm afraid that they might treat us as Japanese. We don't have good Korean friends to rely on, either."

I wished him good luck and came back home right away.

"Mother, is Toru going to stay with Father in the locomotive yard?" I asked.

"Toru has to stay there with Father. Father wants to put all the Japanese people in this city on the Huzan-bound trains, and then he will be on the very last train."

"He thinks he is a captain on a ship?"

"I think so. He is a responsible man."

"How does he know we shall have arrived in Huzan?"

"Don't worry. He tells me that he has the ways to know where we are. He has many Japanese and Korean friends to share and relay the information about us. In other words, he will know where we are. Isn't that nice?"

When Mother, Yoshi, and I were getting ready to leave our house, a woman came to the front door.

"Am I late?"

"Just in time, Yasuko-san," replied Mother.

"Sorry to trouble you!"

"Don't be silly. My husband told me to take good care of you."

Yasuko's husband, Mr. Naito, worked for Father in the locomotive yard. He was also from Shizuoka Prefecture, and Father took special care of him. Yasuko was a lovely thirtyish woman, and I called her Aunty.

When we were about to leave, Mother whispered, "Look! Koreans are already taking a peep into the house. Is it 'first come first served'? We are leaving practically everything behind. Some Koreans are going to be very lucky to have all these things of ours."

"They think they deserve everything, because they think Japanese just came in and took everything away from Koreans," Yoshi said.

"I didn't know that," I admitted.

"Mother, aren't you locking the front door?" asked Yoshi.

"Let's be nice to the new residents whoever may live here. I hope they are going to take good care of our belongings. I left the key on the table in the kitchen." I saw her eyes getting watery.

At that moment, I was recalling something else. I was thinking of the smell that used to come from the paper mill factory, depending on the direction of the wind. I was definitely going to miss the smell of the pulp.

Mother, Yoshi, Aunty Yasuko, and I arrived at Kisshu station at 14:30, as Father had told us to, but Father and Aunty Yasuko's husband were too busy to

August 17, 1945

see us off. The train left at 15:00 for Huzan. When were we going to see Father, Toru, and Mr. Naito again?

38th Parallel Set in 1945

4

THE CITY OF JOSHIN

A few hours from Kisshu Station, our train stopped
chugging south, unable to go farther when it arrived at
the station of Joshin. What happened? We heard that
Russia and America had decided to divide the Korean
Peninsula in half. Russia would control north of the
38th parallel, and America would control south of it.

Trains that happened to be in the north were not
allowed to pass the border to the south, and vice versa.
At that point, all Japanese nationals in North Korea
became refugees, no longer residents. Aunty Yasuko
sighed and said, "We have become refugees after all!"

We heard that the Japanese in South Korea were
moving to Japan via Huzan. They were protected by
our former enemy, the American force. Russia wasn't
our enemy until Japan was about to lose the war. Why

wasn't Russia protecting Japanese nationals in North Korea? Why were these two countries' policies so different? Was it because one was communist, and the other democratic?

As a matter of fact, I didn't even know the word "refugee" until this day. About fifty Japanese were in this train compartment, and we all had become refugees.

A couple days passed on the train. Some Koreans came and went around the train, carrying many kinds of placards.

Go home, Japanese pigs!
We don't need you here in Korea.
Korea, an Independent Nation!
We didn't invite you to Korea.
You invaded Korea.

North Korean Protesters

Among us on this train was a man in his fifties called Mr. Takebe. He was assistant station manager of Kisshu Station, asked by Father to escort Japanese passengers on this train to Fuzan. He knew who we were, and he knew Father remained at the locomotive yard in Kisshu. Mr. Takebe had gone around the city and now brought a piece of good news to us.

"We are going to move to an old Japanese inn instead of staying on this train," he said. "We will live there and see what is going to happen."

About fifty of us refugees walked about half an hour to reach our new living place on a hill. I didn't know how Mr. Takebe managed to find such a deal for us to stay there for free. As the inn didn't have enough rooms for fifty of us, Mr. Takebe arranged for three families, or nine people in total, to stay in the largest room. My family of five would have to share this largest room with Aunty Yasuko and her husband, along with Mr. and Mrs. Takebe. Mr. Takebe believed that Father, Toru, and Mr. Naito, Aunty Yasuko's husband, should be able to join us here in a few days. It would be kind of crowded, but at least we refugees had rooms with roofs to stay in.

Late August 1945

There was a large kitchen to share, and each room had a toilet and a bath. One thing we had to do without was electricity. After the sun went down, we had to rely on the moonlight or candlelight. But I thought we were very fortunate refugees indeed, thanks to Mr. Takebe's efforts.

5

IMPERIALISM AND COMMUNISM

Before we moved to the inn, we had spent three days on the train. There was nothing to do, so I had thought hard about the sudden change in our way of life. First, I had thought about Emperor Hirohito and imperialism.

The first emperor, Emperor Jinmu, was the one who united the different regions of Japan about 2,600 years ago. It was believed that his ancestors were all gods, and therefore Emperor Hirohito was the 124th god-emperor. That is why we had to stand up straight or sit up straight to show our respect whenever we heard the word "emperor."

In school, at the daily morning ceremony, the schoolmaster opened the door of the small, specially made shrine on the stage of the auditorium, and respectfully took out a piece of white paper placed before the large picture of Emperor Hirohito. Printed on the paper was the message from the Emperor on education. Our schoolmaster faced the Emperor's picture to read out the message printed on the paper. Why didn't he turn around, face the students, and read the paper? Because he was not allowed to show his backside to the picture of the Emperor! We all, both students and teachers, had to stand up straight without moving until the schoolmaster finished reading, put the paper back into the shrine, and closed the door.

To tell the truth, the Emperor's words were too difficult for me to understand, so I usually thought of something else while the ceremony was going on:

Does the Emperor fart?
Does he go to the toilet?
Does he think he is one of the gods?
Why must we die for him in the war?
Why must we be killed in the air raid for the Emperor?

Some of the elite graduate students from our school were dying in the Pacific Ocean as kamikaze pilots. They flew their small combat planes down into American warships. Yes, they were suicide fighters. We had banners hanging on the walls of the auditorium that read "Let's follow your senior graduate kamikaze pilot, Mr. So-and-So!!"

Such banners were increasing as days went on. More and more former honor students were dying as kamikaze pilots. Were they willing to die to become so-called military gods for the Emperor? If I had been eighteen or nineteen years old, would I have followed the kamikaze pilots?

After Japan lost the war, the Japanese nationals in Korea lost the right to live in Korea. I was no longer allowed to go to school in Korea. We had to abandon our house and were in the midst of moving *toward* Japan, but we were not allowed to leave North Korea. It seemed we were destined to die out in North Korea. This change was not a natural phenomenon. It was caused by humans. Someone was to blame. But who?

Nothing would be the same as before. The world we lived in before the Emperor's special speech would not be the same afterward. And so I had more questions to wonder about:

Would the national anthem *Kimi-ga-Yo* ("The Emperor's Era") be terminated?

Was Emperor Hirohito going to be the main war criminal?

Was imperialism terminated by American democracy just as the Russian kingdom was terminated by Russian communism?

On the train, I had thought about communism too. I thought how communism and imperialism were alike in the following points:

One person controlled his country for a long time, even decades.

There was no freedom of speech, and human rights were denied.

If there were a weak country nearby, a communist or imperial country's military would invade such a country.

The communist country Russia broke the Goodwill Treaty with Japan right before Japan was about to lose the war against America. Russia then invaded the northern islands of Japan. There was a rumor that Russian war tanks were already coming down from the north into the Korean Peninsula to invade the country.

We heard that those Japanese who lived south of the 38th parallel had started moving down to Huzan to go back to Japan. They were well protected by the democratic country America. Why couldn't the communist country Russia protect Japanese nationals in North Korea?

After the 38th parallel arrangement was made between Russia and America, the government of Russia was surely controlling North Korea. Didn't they care about the Japanese? Why didn't they let the trains with Japanese people on board go through the new border to the south?

I believed that Russia didn't care about humanity. That was communism. I didn't like communism, nor imperialism.

6

BOMBING

As we three families who shared a room at the inn were about to go to sleep, someone suddenly opened the door and called out, "Here we are!" It was Toru.

Father came in next. We expected Mr. Naito to follow. Aunty Yasuko looked for her husband, but she didn't see him. She looked puzzled. Then Father stepped up to Aunty Yasuko and spoke to her.

"Yasuko-san, I'm afraid I have bad news. Your husband was killed in the bombing by Russian planes."

Aunty Yasuko just stood there.

Father continued, "In the evening after you left Kisshu, a few Russian bombers flew over the city and dropped several bombs down onto some important spots, such as the military base, factories, some other spots ... and our locomotive yard, too. A bomb directly hit your husband, and he was killed instantly."

At that, Aunty Yasuko collapsed onto the floor. She was unable to get up for the next two days. She found out that Mr. Naito had been buried by Father and his staff members, deep in the flower garden near his office the next morning.

"I attended the simple burial service," Toru said, "and wanted to put a wreath of flowers on the new grave, but I didn't because lots of beautiful flowers were blooming around there."

Then Toru told us what he had done after the service. "I was curious what had become of our house and went to see it. I knocked on the front door and talked to the Korean man, and I explained that we had lived here before and had forgotten to take the photos with us.

"'Would you let me in and look for them?' I asked.

"'Sure, go ahead.'

"'Thank you! By the way, weren't you afraid of the bombing last night?'

"'Yes, we were. A bomb was dropped near the well in the backyard.'

"'It was? Wow! That must have been scary.'

" 'We were hiding in the shelter. Thanks to your shelter! We appreciate everything your family left here.'

" 'Thanks for saying that! Is the water safe to drink?'

" 'Yes, we can. The roof of the well was blown off, but the well itself was intact.'

" 'That's good. I hope you will live a happy life here.'

" 'Are you heading for Japan?'

" 'I hope so.'

" 'I am praying for your safety! Oh, here is something for you to take to your family. These are Korean mochi made with sticky rice and millet.'

" 'Thank you very much!' "

Toru had left our old house with a handful of our family pictures and the Korean mochi given by the boss of the new residents. He formed the opinion that some Korean people were reasonable and gracious.

7

THE RUSSIAN SOLDIERS

The rumor that Russian forces were getting closer to our area turned out to be reality. A Russian soldier did show up here ... right in our room. The sliding shoji panel suddenly opened, and in stepped a Russian soldier.

The First Russian Soldier

"No!" Father yelled, pointing his finger at the soldier's boots.

The soldier let loose a profanity, shouting *"Davai!"* as he pulled out his pistol, next moment firing it at the ceiling. White powder came down from the white ceiling like rainfall. After the bang, my left ear started ringing.

The Russian soldier pointed the gun at Father's forehead and took Father's wristwatch. Then he took Toru's favorite fountain pen. He next turned to Mr. Takebe, repeating "[Expletive] *davai!*"

Davai must mean "Come on!" or "Please!" or 'Give me—!' in Russian. When Mr. Takebe only shook his head and his hand, the soldier ignored the gestures, snatched the watch off Mr. Takebe's wrist, picked up the alarm clock on the floor, and left our room. It went without saying that he attacked the next room, too.

Mother said to Aunty Yasuko, "I was so scared. I was afraid he might take you away with him. He was staring at you because you are so pretty."

"Oh! No! If he had done so, I would have bitten his arm off," I yelled.

Aunt Yasuko smiled at me.

Russian soldiers were walking around with more than one wristwatch on their arms. Wristwatches and fountain pens were luxury items in Russia? Or were the soldiers on the front a bunch of poor gangs? We had heard that the Russian soldiers who were recently sent down to North Korea were all ex-convicts. Was that why they all had crewcuts?

They even took the large pendulum clock in the lobby, so we had no way to tell the correct time any longer. No wristwatches, no clocks, no alarm clocks! We had to rely on the sunrise and sunset. Were we back to the samurai or ninja era?

After they had taken valuables away from the Japanese here, they just came around to say hello to us. Some brought candies and wanted to have fun with children. Others wanted to teach us simple Russian words while learning easy Japanese words. They even seemed to be friendly. But we heard some "Madam *davai*" stories that had happened somewhere else, though not where we were, thank heaven.

I didn't see any female soldiers. They were always male soldiers. I heard they were looking for women and older girls as they came around saying "Madam *davai*!" I also heard that a Japanese girl had been found dead after being assaulted, and that a Japanese woman had been taken from a public toilet by a few Russian soldiers and later attacked by them.

One late afternoon, such an incident happened here. Our family was out in the backyard. Of course, Aunty Yasuko was with us, too. All of a sudden, a Russian soldier grabbed her by the arm and tried to take her away. Right then, Father cut in between the two and screamed "*Watashino* madam!" Father meant "my woman," and pointing at his nose with his left forefinger, with his right hand he grabbed her by the other arm. The soldier let her go, said something, and went away. Boy, that was close!

Mother said to Aunty Yasuko, "My husband was brave, wasn't he?" and smiled at her.

Aunty Yasuko couldn't stop shaking. She bowed deeply to Father several times.

The Russian soldiers who came around here were mostly young ones. Among them was a tall and good-looking man who was what we might call a familiar face. One day, he brought a loaf of dark Russian bread for our family. I really liked the sort of sourness of the dough, which I had never tasted before. When he brought the same kind of Russian bread again, Mother invited Yashige-san, Ishino-san, and a young man named Taguchi for a bread and tea time. These three had been Father's staff members at the Kisshu Locomotive Yard.

We called the tall Russian soldier *Noppo-san*, which in Japanese means a very tall likable man. Noppo-san taught us easy Russian words. I learned how to say "one, two, left, right" in Russian but didn't know how to write them in the alphabet. Noppo-san also learned how to say those words in Japanese.

"*Ichi, ni, hidari, migi.*" He repeated the words in that order, stomping there. He asked us to join him.

"Ichi, ni, hidari, migi." Taguchi-san, Mother, and I joined the chanting and stomping. Then he gestured, as if he had more food for us somewhere, and signaled us to follow him.

"Ichi, ni, hidari, migi," we kept on chanting, stomping through the yard and out to the road.

It was a nice sunny autumn day with a lovely cool breeze. We walked down the hill to the wide main road. The second or third house from the corner was a shabby old house with the front door unlocked. Noppo-san opened the door, tried to push Mother inside, pointing his gun at Taguchi-san.

"No!" Mother screamed so hard that the passers-by all heard her scream. Taguchi-san turned around and dashed off for help. Mother tried to shake him off, but his hand was too strong.

Suddenly he yelled out a profanity. From behind, a woman had kicked him hard in his leg. Then two other women hit him with parasols on his head and side. The three women were dressed in hanboks, traditional Korean dresses. Noppo-guy had to give up and let Mother go. He left there in a hurry without saying anything. How brave those three Korean women were!

They spoke good Japanese. They said to Mother, "We Korean girls and women are also afraid of Russian soldiers and try not to be alone. Wherever we go, we are with someone." They wanted to escort Mother and me back to the inn.

When we had walked up the hill halfway, Taguchi-san came running down with Yashige-san and Ishino-san.

"These brave ladies saved my life," Mother explained. The ladies said goodbye to us, leaving Mother with the three young men and me. We deeply bowed to them again and again but had no words that could express our gratitude. Mother described them in one sentence: "What a beautiful bunch of Korean ladies!"

One night, something unforgivable happened on the beach nearby. Some Russian soldiers forced several former Japanese soldiers to line up on the waterside then started shooting them. These human targets were all shot to death except one. This soldier from the former Japanese Army was also shot but escaped into the sea—and probably survived, the rumor said.

8

SHERIFFS AND A MOB

While Japan was still in control of Korea, the Japanese police and the Japanese MPs were in charge of the peace. After Japan lost its power over the Korean Peninsula, the sheriff system was born in North Korea.

One day, three sheriffs appeared in the old inn looking for my father. "Are you Takeshi Shimizu?"

"Yes, I am."

"Come with us!" one of them rumbled.

Three hours later, Father returned and collapsed at the shoji screen door. We had no idea what had happened to him. Mother tried to take off his jacket, but his arms didn't move. Father was conscious but unable to talk to her. He just groaned in pain.

Mother then rolled his jacket and T-shirt up to his neck. His back was full of blisters. Without fully taking off his clothes, she applied some grated potatoes over the wounds, which was one of the traditional Japanese ways to supposedly ease pain.

It was obvious that Father was beaten up at the sheriff's office. But why, and what had happened?

The next day, he felt a little better and told us why he had been beaten up. There seemed to be only one reason: the Korean sheriffs wanted to know the location of Father's boss, the director of the Kisshu Locomotive Yard. The director and his Korean wife had disappeared on the day of Japan's surrender to America. Nobody around us knew why the sheriffs wanted to know the couple's whereabouts.

Father, as assistant director, had been at work with both his Japanese and Korean staff members for about a week before he finally left his office, having ensured that his Korean staff would be able to handle the business.

The sheriffs had kept badly beating Father on the back until they were convinced he really didn't know where the director and his wife were. Then they finally let Father go. But it was a good thing his back was the only part of his body attacked, not his face, head, nor other parts. He was escorted right up to the front gate of this place, the old Japanese inn where we were temporarily living.

A couple of months had flown by since we had moved into the old inn. I was still nine years old, and Yoshi twelve. One morning, an unexpected incident occurred.

"What are you guys doing?!"

That was Yoshi's scream. I heard it inside our room. All the adults and Toru were out, and I was the only one there. I opened the shoji screen and looked out to see what was going on. Yoshi was surrounded by several shabby Korean men and women.

Yoshi happened to be taking care of the plants in the garden at the time. The Koreans must have come up the hill beyond the backyard. These Koreans didn't look calm and normal. They held clubs and sticks in their hands.

"OK, let's do it!" someone shouted, and they dashed to the building. "Wahhh!" they yelled.

Strangely, Yoshi wasn't hit. He was only pushed away. "Stop it!" he shouted. Then he chased after two guys who were heading for our room.

I was very scared and went back to my futon. I held my futon and blanket tight. The two guys stepped into the tatami room without taking off their shoes. One guy tried to take away the futon and blanket I was holding, but I didn't let him do it. Yoshi got to the second man from behind, grabbed him by the collar, and pulled it hard. The guy let go of the futon he was holding, and fell down to the hard wooden floor. Yoshi took away the club the guy had and pretended to thrust it at his nose. This guy didn't take anything from our room, but the first guy who couldn't snatch away the futon and blanket from me left the room with Mrs. Takebe's upper futon and her pillow.

The damages in the other rooms were similar to ours. No one was injured. Mostly futons, blankets, and some cooking items were taken away. The Korean mob knew this place had been a Japanese inn and wanted some of the left-behind items. They had no intention to harm us.

9

THE CITY OF KANKO

No ships permitted to leave from North Korea to Japan. The only port that allowed ships to leave for Japan was Huzan in South Korea. That much we knew, thanks to many rumors. We would have liked to be closer to the 38th parallel, where there might be a chance to go across the border into South Korea.

We understood that the border wasn't fenced up or barricaded. If found crossing the border, we would be shot to death by Russian soldiers, but Japanese refugees had somehow been crossing the 38th parallel all the same. The farther south we went, the closer we would get to the border. We had to try to move as far south as possible.

Father and Mr. Takebe somehow arranged for the train to move to the city called Kanko, about a five-hour train ride to the south. We, the fifty or so refugees, boarded the train and arrived at Kanko Station as planned.

When we arrived there, it was drizzling and a bit cold. It must have been almost the end of autumn or the beginning of the winter season. We walked for half an hour and came to an old school building with a large playground.

Late October 1945

There a Korean sheriff with an umbrella was standing on a box-type platform. We gathered before him in the rain—without umbrellas. He started giving a speech in Japanese. He didn't give any instructions or rules for us to follow in order to live in the building. He only preached to us as follows:

We didn't invite you into Korea.

Japan invaded Korea.

The god's country lost the war.

Japan is no longer the god's country.

Emperor Hirohito is the number one war criminal.

Then the sheriff added, "The Korean Peninsula won't be controlled by Japan from now on. The Korean Peninsula is now divided in two, North and South. As the border is not allowed to be crossed, you all must stay here in North Korea until this peninsula becomes one communist nation."

"Excuse me, but may I ask you a question?" one of our men asked him in a loud voice. "How come you don't ship us out of North Korea to Japan?"

"Well, that's because we are not talking to Japan. It will never happen."

"We hear the Japanese citizens in South Korea have been shipped back to Japan from Huzan."

"That's the South Korean business, not ours. I don't care what they do. No more questions! Just follow me to the rooms upstairs."

We followed him into the building and then upstairs. There were two vacant connected rooms by the stairways for us to use. In front of the first room by the stairways, he started counting us as we went up.

"One, two, three … OK, get in this room."

He stopped counting at the twenty-fifth of us and told us to live together … peacefully.

Peacefully?! Did he say that? With twenty-five of us in this former classroom? Without tatami mats on the floor? I was upset, but what could we do? We had no choice in our room or roommates. We were pushed into the first room with Aunty Yasuko but not with Mr. and Mrs. Takebe. They had to follow the sheriff into the next room.

Five Shimizus, one Naito, one Yashige, one Ishino, one Taguchi, one Nakamura, three Kadowakis, three Tomitas, two unknown couples, and five single men were in our room. Mr. and Mrs. Kadowaki had a son who was in his early twenties. I was nine years old but not the youngest. Mr. and Mrs. Tomita had a girl who looked maybe five or six years old.

There was a big question: who would be where? Someone suggested that we decide first where we would like to be. Aunty Yasuko and five of us picked the back left corner of the room. That way we could pile our bags up at the corner. Then the two families of three and the two couples took the spaces by the walls. The five single men decided to stay in the middle of the room, leaving walking space around them. Everyone thought this arrangement should work pretty well.

There hadn't been electricity in the old inn in Joshin, nor there was any in this former school building in Kanko. But that was all right—we knew we could live without electricity. We heard that a hundred other Japanese refugees had been living in the other rooms without electricity since the end of the war.

And this time there was no kitchen. Instead, for cooking there were nearly thirty small U-shaped ovens on the playground. Most of them were made of three rocks or concrete blocks, and belonged to nobody. We could use any one available. This system worked all right for the 150 or so refugees there.

Sleeping Crowded Together

Matches were very precious, and we did not want to waste any of our own. So if one oven was being used, that was good, as any ongoing fire could be shared among other ovens.

However, we had to be very quick as the cooking ground grew crowded before dinner. One time Father chose an available oven, placed old papers and twigs in it, and turned around to reach for the pot and the bottle of water. While he was doing that, the rear concrete block was stolen. He saw a young man walking away with it.

Father ran after and caught him by the collar. "Hey, where are you going with it? Drop it slowly!"

We had to be careful with what we had around, such as twigs and things to be burnt. Those were easily stolen items at the cooking ground.

Water was very precious, too. There were only two faucets for some 150 refugees, one at the east exit and the other at the west exit. There were always some people getting in line to get drinking water during the day.

Outside Cooking Units

10

GHOSTS AND THE HARVEST

"Gyaaah!" I shrieked, ran up the stairways, flew into our room, and landed on some guy's leg. "Ouch! I'm sorry!" I apologized. He didn't say anything. Was I forgiven?

What was I even doing up during the night? I was coming from the toilet downstairs. It was so dark and scary, and I saw a ghost with messy white hair over its face. I was sure I saw only one eye behind the hanging white hair.

Next day on the stairway, I passed an old woman with long white hair. Oh, no! It was her. How cowardly, stupid, and unforgivable! I should have known ghosts don't exist. "I am very, very sorry ... Lady!"

Father's former staff members, Yashige-san and Ishino-san, luckily found jobs at a large farm in the suburb of Kanko as live-in workers. But Taguchi-san suddenly disappeared. I hoped he also found live-in farmhand work, or something similar. Some other single young men were missing, too. There was a rumor that some refugees were taking chances and had succeeded in crossing the 38th parallel. I really hoped Taguchi-san and the other missing young men had had the good fortune to cross over the border.

Nakamura-san was a retired former railroad man. Why didn't he go back to Japan when he retired? Did he like his life in North Korea so much? He was a tall skinny man, and his eyes were always smiling behind his glasses. He liked to go shopping near the street market and buy something to munch on the street. His favorite snack was a flat Korean millet dumpling. It was slightly purple and somewhat sweet. He paid ten yen for mine, too. He didn't want to find a job, so I think he was a rich man with a lot of cash on him, because no banks had been open since Japan lost the war.

The small daughter of Mr. and Mrs. Tomita was always alone in our room during the day. I wanted to talk to her, but I didn't know how to. I grew up with two older brothers and no sisters. Was that why I was unable to talk to her? Anyway, while her parents were out, she played alone in our room. In a way we were all her babysitters. Someone was always looking after her in this large room.

Father and Toru worked together in a rice field. Toru had never worked for a wage before, and the work in the rice field was very hard for him. But he was happy with the job because he got paid as much as Father did. For Father, it was a familiar job, because he used to work in his family's rice fields until he finished elementary school. And then in Korea, his knowledge of threshing had come in handy and surprised the owner of the rice field.

The winter season began, and the rice harvest business was over. Father and Toru were discharged from the farm. But they were told to return there for rice planting the next spring. I was happy for Father and Toru.

While Father was working on the farm, he could bring back bundles of rice straw in order to make straw slippers. I didn't know he could make such slippers. Father taught us how to make them. He told us he had made lots of straw slippers for all his family members when he was growing up in Japan. But straw slippers were not warm enough for the North Korean winter. We decided to save the ones we made for the next summer season.

Mother and Aunty Yasuko were always together. They worked at a large apple orchard. The apple picking season was approaching, and they would be much busier.

Mother said, "It's too early, but we may be able to come back with some apples soon." That was good news. But it was sad not to be able to say "come *home*." No one here had a home to come back to.

Yoshi and I went gleaning. There was not a lot to pick up, and we even picked up ones halfway buried. We walked all over the rice fields for three days.

"I wish these were all sticky rice, but probably not. It's OK, though. After cooking these, I'll pound them in a bowl to make a large piece of substitution mochi," Yoshi said, dreaming of sticky rice cakes and New Year's Day coming up. "And I'll make it flat on the cutting board. It should be sticky enough to make some pieces of rice cake. Ha ha!"

Before that, however, we would have to separate the rice from the rice gleanings. To do that, we put the rice gleanings in a bowl and pounded them until each rice grain came out of each gleaning. When it was done, we blew the empty gleanings away. We had enough rice to be able to make twelve pieces of substitution mocha, two pieces for each of us, including Aunty Yasuko. We would have customary mochi to eat on New Year's Day.

Yoshi and I found very important items in the rice field when we were gleaning. That was a pile of rotten wooden pieces which might have been a part of a farming tool shed or something. The owner of the rice field must have been too lazy to clean them up, so we decided to clean up the mess for him. We bundled them up and carried them on our backs. Yoshi said, "We don't have to buy firewood at the market for a while." We decided to call this spot "our secret base," and went back there from time to time to fuel our oven.

11

SALES AND BEGGING

Yoshi and I were trying to make some imitation mochi with regular rice for New Year's Day 1946, but Toru was planning to make real mochi with *mochi gome*, sticky rice. When he worked with Father in the rice field, he saved the wages and bought the sticky rice for mochi at the Korean market.

Toru made the mochi on New Year's Eve. As we didn't have proper steaming equipment, he had to cook the sticky rice. Then he used a club to pound the cooked sticky rice in a large bowl to make the mochi. Yoshi praised Toru's efforts and the importance of his wages, while I was simply happy for the reality that we would have real rice cakes on New Year's Day. The efforts Yoshi and I made to make imitation mochi wouldn't be wasted, though, because the regular rice we prepared for it would be used in other dishes.

Next morning, Father led the small New Year's Day ceremony with our family and Aunty Yasuko before eating the mochi soup. We said together "Happy New Year!"

And Father added, "We hope the year of 1946 is going to be the year for us to go back to Japan. We must survive this hard winter and wait for a chance to go across the 38th parallel somehow. Let's stay healthy … together!"

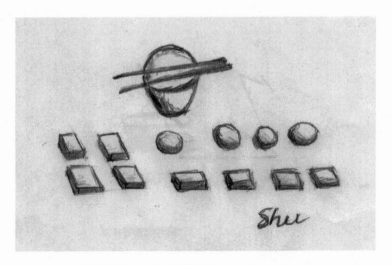

Mochi

When Mother and Aunty Yasuko were at the Korean market soon after, they saw small fresh shrimps and came up with a good idea. They decided to fry the shrimps and make a lot of shrimp tempura to sell to fellow refugees in the old school building.

"Who is going to sell the shrimp tempura?" I asked Mother.

"You will, Shu," Mother said.

"Me?"

"Don't worry! I'm going to be behind you," Aunty Yasuko added.

I had never sold anything to anybody. But Aunty Yasuko would come with me, and then I should be ready to be a shrimp tempura vendor.

Mother and Aunty Yasuko cooked a lot of shrimp *tempura* the next day. I had to sell them before they got too cold. I realized I was in a cold sweat. But I told myself to be brave. I held a tray piled with shrimp tempura. Aunty Yasuko had more shrimp tempura in a bag.

We stood in front of the next room. She knocked on the door and opened it for me. I prayed to god. Then she pushed me in.

"I'm right behind you," she whispered.

"Hello, how would you like shrimp tempura?" My voice wasn't loud enough, I thought.

"Would you like shrimp tempura?" I was able to say it louder this time.

"Six pieces for one hundred yen, or one hundred yen for six pieces, not including these plates."

We didn't have paper bags for them. If we offered bags to put them in, the costs would be more expensive. We didn't want that to happen. The refugees were hungry for Japanese cuisine. Almost all families and even single men bought the shrimp tempura from us, and those pieces that Aunty Yasuko had in the bag were completely sold out before we got to the last room of the building.

"Wow, I did it, Aunty! I mean, *we* did it."

"Yes, you sure did."

I was unable to stop my tears. Aunty Yasuko held my head with her hands and said to me, "I knew you could do it. You were brave!"

"Thank you for supporting me!"

Then I returned to Mother. "Mother, it was a good business! Do you know how much we made?"

"Twenty-four plates ... that's two thousand four hundred yen."

"Two thousand four hundred yen *profit*, Mother?"

"I wish it were. You have to subtract the expenses for the oil and flour and shrimps," Mother said, laughing. And she didn't forget to thank Aunt Yasuko for helping me.

"Did you save some tempura for me to eat, Mother?"

"Oh, no! I forgot! But I still have a lot to sell. How many pieces of shrimp tempura would you like to buy?"

We laughed.

The next idea was Toru's. He already had bought some squashes and agar to make sweet jelly squash, and Yoshi would sell it at the street market. Why Yoshi? Toru said that he himself was the shyest of the three brothers and didn't have guts to sell anything on the street. He told us Yoshi's nature was a merchant type, and it would be good for Yoshi to have some experience. I thought that was only Toru's selfish reasoning.

Toru was quite aggressive. He was positive that this product would sell pretty well. But was it going to be sweet enough? Toru said, "If not, I will add some sugar."

Oh, no! That would be cheating, brother! The squash itself had to be sweet enough.

Toru made some test samples of the sweet jelly squash all by himself, without sugar. Well, was it sweet? Yes, it was surprisingly sweet. He decided not to add any sugar to it. Yoshi tasted it and said "no sugar added" might become a selling point.

Soon Yoshi was sitting at the street market with fifty pieces of sweet jelly squash in a container. Ten pieces of the sweets were placed on top of the lid.

"How about Japanese sweets? Sweet jelly squash! Sugar is not added, but it's surprisingly sweet. And good for your health. And only ten yen a piece." Each piece was nicely wrapped in clear cellophane.

"I want to try one," said a tall Japanese gentleman with a smile on his face.

"Ah! Nakamura-san!"

"Shoo! I'm just a customer. Can I eat it here?"

"Of course, sir."

"Oh, yes! It's not bad at all. Can I have another one?"

Mr. Nakamura became Yoshi's first customer. And other people, Koreans as well as Japanese, bought the sweet jelly squash. From time to time, Yoshi called out the sales pitch, and soon sold out those fifty pieces.

"Well done, brother!" I clapped my hands.

Toru, the shyest of our brothers, broke his invisible barrier of shyness when he started begging for leftover food around the farmers' homes in the suburbs every day.

"We are a family of six, and we are starving. Could you please offer me anything to eat?" said Toru, handing out an empty pot. He brought back some food for us every day. He threw out his Japanese pride somewhere along the way and became a beggar in Korean society. It must have been beyond toleration for him. Very sorry, brother!

Every morning, we heard Russian soldiers singing. Yoshi and I went to the Russian barracks to see what was going on before breakfast. Shortly after we got there, the soldiers' loud chorus was heard. Then a man who looked like a cook

Toru's Begging

came out of the kitchen door with a bucket. There was a fence around the building with a gate. He stepped out of the gate and proceeded toward a large hole where he dumped the contents of the bucket. A few Japanese refugees with empty containers followed him in vain.

They did not get anything from the man who seemed to be a cook. After a while, another cook or a kitchen helper came out with a bucket. This time, one of the refugees got an offering.

That chorus must have been a praying song before their breakfast time. Yoshi and I decided we would come back to the barracks before the Russian soldiers had breakfast. So the next day, we went back there with containers, Yoshi with a cooking pot and me with a *hango*, a vessel especially made for a soldier or a camper to use for camping. We were not the first ones. There were already some adults lined up in front of the gate, so we had to stand at the end of the line. I was at the very end, next to Yoshi.

Hango

Soon we heard the praying song. The soldiers' breakfast began, and a cook came out of the kitchen door with a pail. Walking through the gate, he directly headed to me. He smiled and dumped the contents out of the bucket into my hango. Unbelievable! And he pointed at the ground and said, "Zafutora."

Zafutora, eh? That Noppo-guy, the tall Russian soldier who had almost abducted Mother, had taught me that word. I remembered it meant "tomorrow." He was telling me to come back there the next day. A half loaf of black Russian bread, some pieces of meat, some raw potatoes, and chopped up cheese were dumped into my hango. Wow, they threw away these foods? I wondered. Or had he really wanted to save some uncooked foods and offer them to some poor Japanese? I figured that among those wild Russian soldiers, there was at least one exceptionally kind person!

The next cook with a bucket came out, went through our line, and dumped the contents into the dump hole. And the third one gave some leftover food to Yoshi. The soldiers seemed to select children first. I was still nine at the time, so we both got lucky. We felt kind of sorry for the adults there.

Next morning, we were at the Russian barracks again, of course. The same cook came out and gave me some chopped pieces of fresh food. We decided to go there every other day, and so we did. Mother's work increased because now she had to bake or cook all the foods that were given to us and brought back.

I was given food each time we went to the Russian barracks, but Yoshi wasn't. One morning when he wasn't given any food, he jumped into the dump hole and stood with his pot over his head to wait for food to be dumped. A Russian guard found Yoshi in the dump hole and got so mad that he aimed his revolver at poor Yoshi. Yoshi jumped out of the hole and ran like crazy, chased by the guard until he could disappear into the city.

After we went back to our room, I told our family what had happened to Yoshi that morning. And we burst into laughter!

12

MALNUTRITION, LICE, AND TYPHUS

Toward the end of December 1945, our fellow refugees in the building had started dying with a high fever. It seemed that anyone malnourished was getting this illness and died. The first one to die in our room was the five-year-old girl I have mentioned. Her high fever lasted for three days, and on the fourth day she died. Her parents were also sick, and she wasn't properly attended. The girl's dead body was wrapped in a straw mat and left in the cold corridor for two days.

Father found out there was a mass gravesite for Japanese on the hill to the east of the city. Father carried her body on his back and took her to the grave. A few days later, her parents followed her to heaven. All of a sudden a family of three was gone. This all happened before the New Year's Day when we made the mochi.

Was this illness contagious? Our family had not taken even one shower since we left Joshin, nor had any of the refugees here in this building. We could guess that the illness had a lot to do with lice and malnutrition. Someone found out that this type of illness was called *typhus*. What we could do to face the illness was ... nothing. There were no doctors and no medicine available.

After New Year's Day, the illness, typhus, began raging. Many of our refugees throughout the building started losing their lives. However, the Kadowaki family somehow moved to the nearby Korean hospital. Were they sick? They were so rich that they must have been hospitalized before getting fatally ill, or they had some kind of connection that got them get into the Korean hospital. Unbelievable!

The next typhus victim in our room was Mr. Nakamura. He suffered from a high fever for three days or so, then died very quietly. We took care of him as much as we could, but we couldn't do enough for him without medicine. He left us all the money he had on him, but it was only a few hundred yen. I thought he was a very rich man, but I was wrong.

After Mr. Nakamura died, only thirteen people were left in our room: the five of us plus Aunty Yasuko, two couples, and three single men.

A rumor started going around that the only medicine for typhus—or the only one we had access to, anyway—was the pill bug, a kind of wood louse known for rolling itself up into a ball. And we must swallow at least four live ones as the cure for typhus.

A few days after I heard the rumor about pill bugs, a Korean woman came to our room. Toru paid 300 yen

Pill- Bugs

for twelve pill bugs, then Toru, Yoshi, and I swallowed four live pill bugs each. Eek! And we three brothers prayed hard for a long life.

After someone died, the dead body was taken out of the room and placed in the corridor. The Kanko City Office sent a couple of Japanese men to our building daily to take care of the bodies.

Death

The Japanese body handlers took the dead out to the Japanese communal grave.

The Russian Army finally did something to control the typhus and started a sort of camp to accommodate sick Japanese refugees. I think this place must also have been a former Japanese school. There was a rumor that half the Japanese patients died there, and the other half would be released from there if they recovered.

Yoshi and I got typhus, suffered high fever, but recovered in four to five days. Up to that point, Toru hadn't gotten typhus. I recovered on my tenth birthday, February 9, and I thought I was reborn. Was my life, as well as Yoshi's, saved thanks to those live pill bugs?

Father, Mother and Aunty Yasuko got a fever too, possibly typhus. They lay in their futons, fighting the virus. Then, close to noon, the door suddenly opened without a knock, and a high-ranking Russian soldier with a Korean interpreter came in.

The interpreter said to us, "This officer is a medical doctor, and you are coming with us if you are sick." The Russian doctor pointed at Father, Mother, and Aunty Yasuko. Then the interpreter said, "Those three come with us without anything ... just your bodies."

"Where are you taking us?" Father asked.

"To the rescue camp. It's a place like a hospital," answered the interpreter.

Father, Mother, and Aunty Yasuko stood up to follow the doctor. The interpreter told them to grab only their overcoats. As they were about to go through the door, Father turned around and said to me, "Shu, you have some fever. Come with me. Get your heavy coat. It's cold out."

"Me? I don't have a high fever, Father!"

"You sure do. Just come with me."

Father's command was absolute. I put on my overcoat.

When we stepped out of the room, Father turned around again, opened the door, and tried to talk to Toru and Yoshi. He said nothing, nothing at all. He couldn't say anything, but his eyes seemed a little wet.

A few minutes later, about twenty Japanese refugees were on the cart pulled by a couple of horses. The cart was built from wood panels, but the wind blew through the gaps between the panels. It was exactly one week after my tenth birthday. We left for the rescue camp on February 16, 1946.

About fifteen minutes later, we reached the camp. Our chances were 50–50, if the rumor that the survival rate was 50 percent was right. We had to survive somehow. I would be leaving here with Father, Mother, and Aunty Yasuko, or four of us together.

13

THE RESCUE CAMP AND FATHER'S DESTINY

When we reached the rescue camp, there were two entrances side by side. Father and I were to go in through the left door, and Mother and Aunty Yasuko through the right one. We stripped ourselves, and our clothes were separately wrapped in paper bags with our names. Then we got haircuts, and Father's hair in his armpits and crotch was cut with a clipper.

Then we went into the steamy bathroom. We were told to wash our body thoroughly in the shower before jumping into the large bath in the middle of the room. Several naked men were in the heated water. I felt so good in the hot water and didn't want to get out of the bath. But all those men, including Father, were suffering from high fever and couldn't stay in as long as they wanted to.

After Father and I got out of the bathtub, we were permitted to wipe our bodies with large bath towels but had to give them back to the attendant in charge of towels. We were told to go out of the room naked. Father didn't have any hair on his head, in his armpits, between his thighs, or on his legs. The hair had been clipped off from his entire body.

"Eh, don't we get pajamas or gowns to wear?" Father asked.

"Outside the door, please!" came the answer from the Japanese male attendant.

We went out of the room at the same time Mother and Aunty Yasuko were coming out of the door next to ours. They were stark naked, without any hair on their heads and between their thighs. It seemed like a reunion of five babies together face to face ... now free of lice.

We were met by a male Japanese clerk and a female Japanese clerk who handed us yukatas, light kimonos. Mine was too big for me, but that meant I could easily cover my whole body with it. Mother and Aunty Yasuko were escorted to the women's ward on the second floor, and Father and I were taken to the men's ward on the ground floor. Our beds were placed side by side. There were eighteen more beds, all occupied by Japanese patients.

The windows were barricaded with iron bars like a jail cell so that the patients couldn't escape. In addition to the twenty beds in our ward, there was a stove. No lights. There were windows close to the ceiling above the regular windows, and the room was light enough to move around at night. Whenever bright moonlight shone through those upper windows, I thought it was so pretty. I didn't mind living without electricity during the night. I must have become used to the darkness.

The same Russian doctor came around once in the morning and never showed up the rest of the day. There was no medicine nor shots, and no drip infusion. This was not a hospital but a place to gather Japanese typhus patients. That was all. If we were lucky, we would survive. If we were not lucky, we would die.

There was a Japanese woman assigned to this room to take care of the patients. We called her Tanaka-san. And she saw through that I was not sick at all. I told the truth to her—that as Father didn't want to be alone and lonely, he had told me to accompany him. I also told her about Mother and Mrs. Yasuko in the women's ward upstairs. She told me not to worry. She predicted I would leave this place with Father, Mother, and Aunty Yasuko.

Tanaka-san came around every morning to each bed to take our temperature. If we recovered and the normal temperature lasted more than three days, we would have to leave. She promised to cheat on my temperature and every morning wrote down 38.0°C to 39.0°C on her temperature sheet to hand to the Russian doctor. My normal temperature was 36.3°C (97.3°F), and at the rescue camp was about the same every morning. I knew the normal temperature of Japanese people ran from 35.5°C (95.9°F) to 37.4°C (102.2°F), but Tanaka-san was willing to lie for me on her temperature sheet.

Day and night, I heard groaning and yelling all over the room. One man suffered from frostbite on both of his legs besides typhus, and the air in the room was terribly smelly. He died two days later, and two other men died of typhus, one after another. It didn't take long for the empty beds to be filled with new patients. More people seemed to be leaving this rescue camp dead than alive.

Father's fever didn't go down. Instead it was getting worse. On the third day he was unable to eat. At night he began calling the names of his wife and sons, though not mine. He repeated *Suzuko, Toru, Yoshi; Toru, Suzuko, Yoshi; Suzuko, Toru,* and so on. The order of the names he called was not the same. He didn't have to call me because he knew I was right by him, holding his hand.

The darkness of the night was getting a bit lighter. It was before sunrise. Father finally looked like he was dozing off, so I went back to my bed to take a rest.

"Shu, water ... water, please!" Father's voice woke me up. Then I saw our caretaker Tanaka-san walking around in the room, already on duty.

"Tanaka-san, could you bring some water for my father, please?" I asked her.

"No problem, Shu-chan." *Shu-chan* was like "Master Shu," with some affinity because I was still a child. Tanaka-san raised Father's head a little and helped him drink some water. I thanked Tanaka-san.

When I was eating breakfast on my bed, I heard Father clearing his throat. I moved to his bed and saw him taking a big breath.

"Father ..."

That was the last time I called him "Father" in his presence. He died February 20, 1946, the fourth day after we came to the rescue camp. I had never imagined he was so close to dying. He wasn't rescued. He became one of the unfortunate 50 percent.

He had forced me to come with him. Was it because he dared to choose the destiny to die with me by his side? Did he select me because he loved me most?

"Oh, Father! I love you!" I cried under the blanket on my bed.

Father's body was carried out by two Japanese attendants. His bed was cleaned and prepared for the next patient.

The next day, a young man was brought in and assigned to Father's bed. He was not heavily sick, and we started talking a lot. As we talked, I noticed an apparent scar in his left palm. I asked what happened to his left hand, and as he replied, I soon realized that he was recounting the incident on the beach at Joshin, the night the Russians had used Japanese soldiers as human targets.

"Wow, you were the one who escaped into the sea ... and survived!?"

"Yes, I was lucky. God saved me!"

"I am very, very happy for you! You were so brave!"

"Thanks! I'm going to live forever! Ha ha!"

And the two of us laughed together. So the rumor we had heard about the human targets in Joshin was true, and so was the legend of the soldier who escaped into the sea!

Tanaka-san brought me a piece of good news. Mother would be ready to leave the rescue camp in three days, and Tanaka-san would adjust my daily temperatures accordingly to report to the Russian doctor. She would take me to the women's ward in order to meet Mother so that we could leave this place together.

The day of discharge finally came. This place was not a hospital, so the word "discharge" might not be accurate. Anyway, I could leave this place with Mother and Aunty Yasuko.

Tanaka-san escorted me to the women's ward upstairs. Soon Mother came out of the room ... alone. I dashed into her arms and cried, "Mother, Father is gone. Father died!"

"Ugh! Father is dead?! Tanaka-san didn't talk about him, and I was guessing the worst case, but ..."

"Aunty can't leave here yet?"

"She died, too!"

We held each other and kept crying.

"OK, then," Tanaka-san finally said. "Let's go get your clothes. Please come with me." We followed her to the locker room downstairs.

Mother and I walked quickly hand in hand, retracing the way the two-horse wagon had taken us to the rescue camp until we reached the old school building we had been living in.

"Toru and Yoshi! We are back … without Father and Yasuko-san," Mother greeted them.

"Mother, we know," said Toru. "Father's former staff members came by from the Japanese community grave. They were working for the rescue camp and took Father's body to the grave. They were unable to bring anything but his cut eyebrow, cut finger nail, and his round eyeglasses. He was naked and had no hair on his body."

"Aunty died, too," I said, holding deep emotion in my heart. I didn't want to cry again.

"Mother, you must be immortal. You didn't even swallow those creepy live pill bugs, did you?" said Yoshi.

"Ha ha! You will never die, Mother!" I added. Then we all laughed.

"Father left enough money for us to live for another year or so," Toru said. "We must survive this hard winter somehow. Let's stay healthy, then we must go back together to Father and Mother's hometown in Shizuoka."

Toru had become the head of the Shimizu family, now that Father had died.

In the beginning of April, Taguchi-san was found dead in the space behind the stairways at the old school where we had been living. Where had he been? Did he die of typhus, too? He looked extremely thin, but his face didn't show any pain or suffering. I hoped Taguchi-san was met by Father and Mr. Naito in heaven.

14

SPRINGTIME

Yoshi and I kept going to the Russian barracks to get their food scraps or leftover food. Toru went around the wealthy residential area, asking for food or jobs or anything he could do. Once he was able to work for a whole day helping a family with yard work. We brothers asked Mother to keep an eye on what we had, since our belongings were not hidden or locked in our room.

At the end of March, the cold was getting a bit easier to bear. And at the beginning of April, the sun started to come out more often, making it easier to spend the days outside. When the wind was not blowing at all, and the sunshine was warm and comfortable, some of our male refugees sunbathed, leaning against the building wall. Others shook the lice off their clothes over the ongoing ovens, and enjoyed the sound of the lice being burnt in the fire. Yoshi and I did the same, and found that this was the best method to kill the lice. We even stripped to our underpants to perform the small ceremony of killing the creepy little enemies.

One sunny day, we three brothers went out to catch fish in a brook we knew running by the rice paddies. Father had shown Toru how to catch fish in the brook when they worked together last fall. A bamboo basket was used to catch fish.

Toru stepped in the brook first. The water was still very cold, so we took turns going into the water. The fish we caught were mostly loaches, small bottom-dwelling freshwater fishes. Other fish were too small, and we let them go. We caught a dozen loaches.

As we were about to leave, suddenly we were surrounded by several Korean boys.

Fighting?

"Hey, what do you think you're doing? You're stealing Korean fish. You guys are thieves," said the tallest boy, who was about Toru's age. He swung his fist at Toru, but Toru was fast enough to dodge it. At the same time, Toru grabbed this boy's collar and elbow. They didn't move a bit for a while.

"Hmm, you know judo, eh?"

"I sure do."

"Well, then. I don't want to fight with you." The tall Korean boy stepped back and bowed. "Judo is not for fighting. I was taught that way. Sorry!" The Korean boys turned around and went away.

"Eh?" I couldn't believe it. "Judo's lesson is a lesson for controlling your mind, too? That's amazing."

Our surroundings in the city of Kanko began changing in late April. The city was getting greener and brighter. More people were out walking, a bit slower and even looking happier. We refugees at least had more things to eat—young soft greens. Yoshi and I went around the countryside and picked all kinds of "weeds" whose names were unknown to us. Mother cooked them with rice and dried cod filets. The cod had some salty taste, and those greens gave flavor to it. It didn't taste great, but it was edible and nutritious.

One day Mr. Takebe next door came to visit us. He said, "I have arranged a freight train to go down to the south, which has room for fifteen people or so. We can go to a beach town called Bunsen about seventy kilometers south. That's as far south as we can possibly go. But we may have a chance to walk across the 38th parallel. We will be walking about twenty kilometers a day for ten days. After crossing the border, within a few kilometers' walk, we should be able to get to the American Marine base in a city called Bunsan. Would you come with us?"

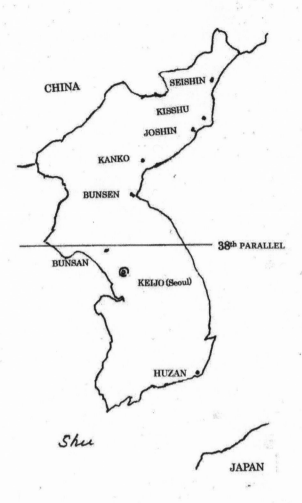

CHINA

SEISHIN

KISSHU

JOSHIN

KANKO

BUNSEN

38th PARALLEL

BUNSAN

KEIJO (Seoul)

HUZAN

Shu

JAPAN

Bunsen to Bunsan

"Yes, we would, Takebe-san," said Toru without asking Mother.

"Four of us, and can you take two more young men?" Toru continued. "I want to get Yashige-san and

Ishino-san, who used to be Father's staff members. They now live and work in a large farming outfit."

"Oh, I know them. They are fine young fellows. Done! Altogether, fourteen of us will be heading for freedom in a week."

"Takebe-san, did you say we will start walking from Bun*sen* to Bun*san*? It's so confusing," I said.

"Yes, it is confusing. But don't worry. Just follow me. I'll take you to Bunsan.

The next day, Mother and Toru walked to the large Korean farm to talk to Yashige-san and Ishino-san. The young men were so glad, and Ishino-san said to Mother, "Thank you so much for the exciting news. We will be thrilled to take the chance with the late assistant director's family. He will be protecting us all the way to South Korea from heaven."

"And to Japan!" added Yashige-san.

A couple of days later, they were able to leave the farm and come to our room. The following day, we all went to the Japanese mass gravesite. Toru remembered that Father's grave number was 11, as he had been told by the young men who had taken Father's body to the site. The number eleven grave was halfway up the eastside hill. It was already covered with rounded, piled-up soil.

Yashige-san and Ishino-san knelt and joined their palms together. Mother, Toru, and Yoshi joined the two. I did the same and prayed for Father and Aunty Yasuko. Aunty, I thought, must have died around the same time as Father, and so she must be in this grave with Father and unknown Japanese men, women, and children all together. *I am leaving this city of Kanko tomorrow*, I said in my prayer. *Sayonara, Father and Aunty Yasuko!*

15

STARTING POINT FOR FREEDOM

Fourteen of us refugees—Mr. Takebe's group of eight plus the six of us—boarded the freight train as he had arranged. We could sit on the freight, the boxes, baskets, and so on. It took about two hours to get to Bunsen, which was a small town facing the Sea of Japan. From Bunsen in North Korea to the 38th parallel, we would be walking 160 kilometers, almost a hundred US miles. From the 38th parallel to the American military base in the city of Bunsan, South Korea, the distance might be a couple more kilometers. The distance was estimated in a straight line on the map, but we would be walking up and down, left to right, right to left, zigzagging, and might have to walk considerably more than 160 kilometers, all together, in ten days or so.

After getting off the freight train in Bunsen, we happened to come to a large parklike place. Mr. Takebe decided to sleep there for a night and depart early in the morning. But a Korean woman came to tell him something serious. She said, "I heard a couple of sheriffs planning this. You all might be taken somewhere on a truck tomorrow morning. I don't know the purpose. In the past, a Japanese group was taken away by Korean sheriffs, and no one knows what has become of the group. You might be facing danger."

So Mr. Takebe changed his plan and told us to take a good rest right then. Then he added, "As soon as it gets dark and the town gets calm, we will be sneaking out of this town very quietly."

Then some went shopping, and others had an early dinner in town. Japanese yen was still good to use.

Afterward, Takebe-san came around and indicated that we would be leaving soon. He told us that the group was down to twelve people. The elderly couple was missing. They had left a note on Mrs. Takebe's bag and disappeared. The note said that they were too old to go with us. They did not want to be trouble to our group. The letter ended by wishing us success in crossing the border. It was a sad case, but we had to get going without the elderly couple. I wished for an easier life for them in North Korea.

When we left Bunsen, it was eight o'clock at night. We kept on walking through the first mountain and a forest, and then came to the foot of the second mountain. There, we stopped for our first rest and a snack time at three o'clock in the morning. It was my first such experience, and I kind of liked it. After a short rest, we started walking again. We followed passages like animal trails, the paths only hunters or mountaineers might use, and lanes between fields, never through a paved road. We also walked along a stream.

Sneaking Out of Bunsen

We didn't stop for breakfast, and finally stopped for late lunch at the third mountaintop. We figured that that no Korean sheriffs were around, for sure. It was three o'clock in the afternoon. After a thirty-minute lunch break, we decided to walk on down the mountain, then we would see what happened. We were very tired and wanted to go to sleep early.

We happened to reach a small village at sunset. Takebe-san went to look for a place where twelve refugees could lie down. He knocked on the door of a house that looked like a farmer's residence. His insight proved right. There was a shed for farming equipment with enough room for twelve people to lie down to go to sleep, and we were allowed to use their toilet outside.

The owner of the house said to us, "There are so many people who feel sorry for Japanese refugees. There are many things we owe to Japan and Japanese people. Japan introduced some modern culture to Korea. The three main things are the large dam, the railways, and main wide roads all over the peninsula. I'm sorry you have to leave Korea in this way."

I was awakened abruptly by Toru. "Shu, wake up! Everybody is getting ready to leave."

"I'm sorry, but I am tired," I said.

"Everyone is tired, but we must get going," said Yoshi.

I tried to get up, but my legs wouldn't move. I was unable to move my legs! They didn't feel like my own legs. What happened to my legs? I wanted to go to the toilet, but I couldn't get up. Crawling was all I could do—barely. I crawled, crawled to the outside toilet. Yoshi came to help me stand up to urinate. Holding onto Yoshi's shoulder, I was barely able to move my stiff legs forward. That was not walking at all.

Mother was waiting for me at the gate of the farmer's house.

"Mother, my legs are like a pair of crutches. I can't move them."

"They are gone. Come on, Shu, walk!" said Mother.

On our first day, we had started out at eight o'clock in the evening and walked for seven hours, until three in the morning. After a short snack, we had walked for another seven hours or so, then around ten in the morning had brunch by a narrow river and rested well. After that, we walked five more hours, until sunset. In total, we had walked for nineteen hours in two days without sleeping. I was the youngest among our twelve refugees. On the third morning of our march to the 38ᵗʰ parallel, I wanted to be forgiven. My ten-year-old legs were too tired.

"Shu, please move your legs. I must take you to Father's house where he was born."

"I was born in Korea. Keijo is my hometown, Mother. I can't walk. I want to stay here. Please leave me here. I'll be a Korean boy," I cried, shedding tears in big drops.

On the Second Day

"But you're Japanese, and you must move to Japan. You are not allowed to live in Korea any longer because Japan lost the war, Shu."

"I don't understand that, Mother!"

Mother pulled me much harder, and my body flipped over. Then Yoshi helped me stand up straight and pushed me forward from behind.

Then a strange thing happened. My legs moved. The numbness in my legs suddenly disappeared. I felt like my legs were getting electricity or energy.

"Mother, my legs felt some kind of electricity, and the numbness is gone now. I think I can walk!"

"Father must have given you the electricity!"

Toru came back to see how I was doing. "They are waiting for you up there," he said. "We must hurry."

At times we had to go through villages and towns. We were hoping we would not see any Korean sheriffs, but it was inevitable. Each time we were found by them, we had to open the bags and boxes we had on the ground. The worst cases were when women were called in to their offices, and the doors were closed. Both Mrs. Takebe and Mother experienced such an ordeal one day. They were called into the sheriff's office together and had to take off their outer clothes. They had paper money sewn into their collars. The collars were cut open, and the money was all taken away by the Korean sheriffs.

But I had paper money safely hidden in my canteen. I also carried our money in a bundle of vegetable leaves and inside weeds. The money I had with me was never found by the sheriffs.

Sheriff's Inspection

Once when we were walking near a village, three Korean boys came to me and said, "Hello, aren't you hungry? You must be very hungry. We will give you this."

One of the boys had something hidden behind his back. "Here!" said the boy, and thrust out a snake right before my face.

"Gyaaah!" I screamed and ran off to Toru. The boys came after me.

Toru saw the snake and struck it down with his walking stick. It was dead, but I had never seen a real snake in my life. So I was frightened.

"Snakes are 'delicious' and good eating," the boy shouted, then ran away with the two other boys, leaving the dead snake there.

Then why didn't they pick it up and take it with them to eat? Did they just want to startle me? However, I learned one thing: snakes *are* good to eat, and Korean people eat snakes. If I had known how to prepare and cook the snake, maybe I would have kept it as a delicacy.

We slept by a brook, on a hill, in a forest—anywhere we could hide ourselves. When we were able to sleep inside someone's house or barn, we felt very lucky. The kindness of a property owner might protect us from bad weather or wild animals, and his warning from possible harm by bandits—or Korean sheriffs.

Once we were able to sleep in one of the rooms owned by an elderly man, who almost certainly averted a danger to us. Unknown to us, after we went to sleep a visitor came. This visitor was a Korean sheriff who ordered the owner of the house not to let us go anywhere. "I will be back in the morning," the sheriff said to him.

This sympathetic old man suspected something fishy and woke Mr. Takebe. Within fifteen minutes, we set out walking fast and disappeared into the forest. Thanks to the old man, we remained free. But what would happen to him when the sheriff came back and found out we were gone? I was guessing he would pretend that he wasn't aware of us sneaking out of his house.

We rushed through the forest and into the next mountain. After we passed the top of the mountain and started going down the slope, an accident happened. Mother slipped and slid down the slope for nearly two meters, landing on her tailbone.

"Ugh!" She was in terrible pain and unable to move.

"No problem. We will take turns and carry you, Oku-san," Yashige-san said, using the polite form of address for someone's wife. "I'll carry you first. Then Ishino will carry you."

Mother had lost some weight during the last several months and wasn't heavy. But if these young men hadn't been with us, that might have been the end of her. We were thankful that their former boss—Father— must have been such a good boss to them. I was so appreciative of Yashige-san and Ishino-san. While Yashige-san was carrying Mother, Ishino-san had to carry Yashige-san's belongings, and vice versa.

Takebe-san understood the situation, and his group slowed down a little because of Mother's injury. She kept saying "I'm sorry" to other group members. That night, we had early dinner on the hillside, rested well, and slept there. That was Takebe-san's thoughtful idea so that Mother could rest and recover sooner. And by the next morning, Mother was able to walk slowly. Hurray, Mother! We would get going!

Mother always had salt in her pocket. When I was getting tired or too thirsty, she put some salt on my palm. I walked, licking the salt little by little. Salt strangely worked on me. Another thing Mother did to encourage me was to sing the very famous Japanese song that was taught in school. It was like a marching song, with that kind of beat, praising the steep and rugged Mount Hakone. Mother and I happily sang the song together and marched forward.

On the afternoon of the tenth day, a Korean man in his forties approached us quietly. He looked as if he had been waiting for us. He said, "You guys are getting very close to the border line, the 38th parallel, and should know many things before crossing the border. How would you like to choose me as your border guide? Please come to my house. I will explain the details there."

We followed the man to his house. We were offered some tea with the Korean pickles we called *kimuchi*. Could we trust him? He looked earnest. Takebe-san searched his group members' faces for approval and decided to go with this man to the 38th parallel.

Our newly selected Korean guide kept talking.

"OK, then. I'll explain. There is a river at the 38th parallel. When you cross the river, you don't need anything. All you need is your own body. You shouldn't be carrying things. The lighter, the better. Once you cross the river, soon you will be rescued by ... South Korean people and the American military. You will be taken to Huzan by train. Then you will be taken to Japan on a Japanese ship arranged by the Japanese government, free of charge. The train fees for your hometown will be paid by the Japanese government too. You won't need any money. So please leave me the money on you now. That money will be the guide fees for me to take you to the 38th parallel. You leave your pots and pans, blankets, futons, bags, and so on with me."

Our twelve refugees discussed for a while and came to the conclusions: We would give all the money we had on us to this Korean guide, and leave every belonging we had with us in his house. We bet our lives on this Korean gentleman. We had to believe he was deeply trustworthy and truly sincere. The money that paid for our lives was piled up on a large tray, and our belongings were placed on the floor of the room.

"And one more thing you must leave here is your cane or stick," he continued. "One place is a critical point where you must walk step by step, sideways like a crab, and hand in hand using both of your hands. I'll hold this boy's left hand with my right hand, and his mother will hold his right hand with her left hand, and so on. You got it? We have to move that way for about forty meters."

"We must be walking on … what?" asked Takebe-san.

"It's a concrete divider like a wall. That's all you have to know. If we are very careful, we can go through this critical point. Then, soon you will come to the river which we call 38th parallel."

We followed our newly hired man who hopefully would be the last human being we would see in North Korea. We walked through the woods and came to what this guide had called the "critical point." He called for me and held my left hand, then told me to hold Mother's left hand with my right hand. Mother's right hand held Yoshi's left hand, and Yoshi's right hand held Toru's left. Next was Yashige-san, then Ishino-san, and so on. The last person was Takebe-san with his cane.

We moved to the left, side by side, and soon we went into something like a tunnel. Suddenly, we were walking in complete darkness. We could hear some water running. It sounded like a small canal or drainage. The Korean guide walked to the left, pulling us, the twelve Japanese refugees, to the left. It was so strange that he hadn't told us what we would be walking through. We moved slowly and very carefully, hand in hand to the left, like a row of crabs. I was scared and felt my heart pounding very fast. *We must be walking on top of a high wall where water is running below. If we fall off the wall, we might die,* I thought.

Whew! We came through the "critical point" without problem.

"Now to the 38th parallel," whispered the guide. We walked about two kilometers and stopped at the bank of the river, the 38th parallel border.

"This is it. You decide when to cross the river … without being found by the Russian army. Good luck to you all!" the guide murmured to us.

He lay down to rest in the bushy area before the river bank. We did the same.

After a time, we heard a couple of dogs bark somewhere, far away in the distance. We looked in the direction of the barking, then suddenly lights came on. Oh, no! It was a Russian barracks. They had found us! At the same time, a couple of trucks drove into the Russian military base. The distance to the base was about 200 meters. We had to be dead quiet.

Someone whispered that the guide was nowhere in sight. He had gone. He did what he had to do, then disappeared without saying goodbye. He didn't want to get into any trouble or get shot to death with us, I guessed.

16

THE 38TH PARALLEL

It seemed around two o'clock in the morning. Takebe-san said in a very low but firm voice, "Get ready. We go over the bank and cross the river. I checked around the river earlier and found out there are about ten narrow wooden boards connected across the river. You can imagine an old narrow wooden bridge. We have to walk on each board one by one. This bridge-like thing might be very fragile. Even if you fall into the river, don't panic. You can walk across the river. I think the current is very calm. Beyond the river, there is the free world you've been dreaming of. Are you ready? OK? Let's go!"

Crawling up the bank, we followed Mr. and Mrs. Takebe and stepped down to the river. Takebe-san told me to get on the wooden board first, and Yoshi, Toru, and then Mother. Takebe-san was the last one to get on the board.

The wooden board swung up and down a little, but I was able to step onto the next board. Each panel was supported by a few spikes under the board. We walked smoothly on the board, and no one fell into the water. This bridge-like walkway must have been built long before the Korean Peninsula was divided in half. The river happened to be at the 38th parallel. I was grateful to the people who had built this walkway so that eventually the Japanese refugees could escape from North Korea to South Korea.

After everyone had crossed the river, we climbed the bank and ran across the wild field and through the rice paddies, where we came to another field. We were so tired and had to take a rest. We dropped down to the ground. This had to be the soil of South Korea at last. Some of the refugees kept kissing the soil, and so did I.

Breaking Dawn of Freedom

The sun was trying to show its face. "Look, the sun is coming up!" I said. That was the beginning of our very first day in the free world. It happened on May 11, 1946, nine months after we abandoned our house in North Korea.

We started walking again toward the south. My legs didn't feel tired. We were striding away. Then a few Korean farmers came upon us. "Welcome to South Korea!"

"Are you sure we are in South Korea?"

"You bet."

"Banzai!" *Hurrah*, every one of us said. "Banzai!"

"Go this way, and you will come to the US Marine base. You will be rescued there. About two kilometers to the base."

"Thank you very much!"

We thanked the farmers again and again.

We couldn't wait to feel or taste some kind of freedom we had dreamed of. The two kilometers seemed way too far. We walked steadily but fast, and soon we were standing in front of the main gate of the US Marine base. An American flag was flying from the highest point of the building. At the gate, a tall white soldier was standing straight with a rifle. When we stepped forward and got close to the guard, he saluted us.

I was thinking how this American soldier saluted these shabby-looking Japanese refugees who in appearance were exactly like beggars or the homeless. Had I experienced this kind of treatment from Russian soldiers in North Korea? Hardly! Here we were treated like respectable humans. This must be the world of democracy, I thought.

The marine smiled and gestured for us to go into the gate. We were met by another soldier, who was a young black woman. She escorted us to a room where we all were sprayed from head to toe with white powder called DDT. Our damned lice were all killed right there. We showered and those who needed them were given new underwear, clothing, and shoes.

Then we had a physical examination. The doctor was Japanese. He said, "I'm here waiting for my family. I happened to be in one of the southern cities when the 38th parallel was set. My family was in North Korea then. I am going to be here until they get to this point."

I prayed from the bottom of my heart for his family's safety.

In the evening, we had a bonfire in a former theater without any seats. Right at the middle of the floor, the fire was built up, and potatoes and sweet potatoes were baked for us.

"If only Father could eat this potato here with us!" cried Mother. I saw her cry for the first time since I had told her about Father's death. I was also thinking of the late Aunty Yasuko.

After the first "hotdog and salad" dinner I'd had in my life, we were given sweet potatoes again for supper, and cushions and blankets to sleep in. We were treated like special guests.

Next morning, we were sent on a truck from the marine base in Bunsan to Keijo Station some fifty kilometers away. I saw American soldiers also being carried on their military trucks. When our military truck passed their trucks on the way, American soldiers waved at us, knowing we were Japanese refugees.

Now we were at the railroad station of Keijo, today known as Seoul. We were going to be put on a train to Huzan, where we would board a Japanese ship and then depart from the Korean Peninsula for Japan. Under the North Korean soil we were leaving Father, Mr. Naito, Mrs. Naito (Aunty Yasuko), Nakamura-san, and Taguchi-san, among countless dead Japanese people. I prayed for them to sleep in peace.

Did I not wish to go back to Father's grave in North Korea? My answer is no ... not until North Korea becomes a democratic country with freedom or democracy as its principles.

Under imperialism, Japanese citizens had no choice but to obey and die for the Emperor. After the Emperor surrendered to America, the Japanese nationals in North Korea were not protected by the Emperor nor by the Japanese government. Under communism, the

Japanese were not protected in North Korea and were still dying there.

Under democracy, all the Japanese in South Korea had been given freedom and sent back to Japan. Every Japanese national who came into South Korea, or would come into South Korea in the future, would be given freedom and sent back to Japan.

After having been disappointed in Imperialism and Communism in North Korea, I was given freedom in South Korea under the American way of democracy. I should say that I saw a new light escaping from North Korea into South Korea.

Arigato!

Acknowledgments

After escaping from North Korea to South Korea, I grew up in Shizuoka Prefecture, my parents' birthplace. After finishing my high school education at Shimizu Higashi High in Shizuoka Prefecture, I worked through two colleges. First, I graduated from Waseda University in Tokyo, majoring in journalism. Then I graduated from San Diego State College, California, majoring in speech arts. I went through two colleges because my father used to tell us, his three sons, "You must finish college." He had only an elementary school education and had huge disadvantages in climbing up the career ladder in Japanese and Korean railroad companies. But I think I can say that I faithfully followed my father's advice ... twice.

While attending SDSC, I started working for American Airlines in San Diego and retired at its headquarters in Dallas, Texas, after having been with the company for twenty-eight years. That's why I have many friends in America.

Of my older two brothers, Yoshi graduated from Tokyo Economic University, taking night courses while working for Hino Diezel Company. But the company refused to recognize his night school credentials, so he left the company in disgust. He joined a Yamasa Fish Cake Company in the city of Toyohashi in Aichi Prefecture and retired as executive director at age seventy. His son, Akira, graduated from Keio University, and Akira's two daughters graduated from Azabu Veterinarian University and Waseda University. My father's wish was fulfilled by his son, grandson, and great-granddaughters.

After finishing high school, my big brother Toru started working in order to support us as the head of our family, taking a job with a newspaper company in the city of Toyohashi. While he was working, he finished Hosei University's correspondence course. He worked for two newspaper companies and twice became director in chief. Afterwards, he worked as chief secretary for the Minister of Education and Science in the Diet (parliament) in Tokyo. Toru's son and grandson both graduated from Tokyo University. Toru's childhood dream of getting into Tokyo University was fulfilled by his descendants.

When Toru was a journalist, he wrote a book on the same subject matter as mine. I have borrowed some illustrations from his book for this memoir. He passed away two years ago, and I had to get permission from his son to use them. I am sure Toru would let me use them if I could ask him. Our mother passed away twenty years ago, long before Toru's death.

One person I should include here is my teacher's father, Mr. Miyajima, who was abducted by Koreans in Kisshu right after the end of the war in 1945 (described in chapter 3, "Farewell"). He was still missing in 1960. I found out my teacher lived in Tokyo, and I was able to visit her before I left Japan to go to study at San Diego State College. She told me then that she suspected her father had been killed by Korean mobs.

Finally, I must include my gratitude to Ms. MaryJane Stubbs Themudo and Ms. Joy Mungovan Savage, who were my superiors and friends at the headquarters of American Airlines in Dallas, Texas. To bring out this book at this time, I needed their advice and encouragement, and they even offered to proofread the manuscript. I owe them a great deal, which I could never repay in my life. My gratitude goes also to my friend and PC specialist Yurie Murai, who spent many hours assisting me with PC works. I cannot possibly put my thanks into words for these three ladies. Without MaryJane, Joy, and Yurie there would be no book.